ANIMAL OPPOSITES
BIG AND SMALL

by Cecilia Minden

Cherry Lake Publishing • Ann Arbor, Michigan

1

Published in the United States of America
by Cherry Lake Publishing
Ann Arbor, Michigan
www.cherrylakepublishing.com

Reading Adviser: Marla Conn, ReadAbility, Inc.

Photo Credits: © Heidi Schneider/Shutterstock Images, cover, 20;
© Victoria Rak/Shutterstock Images, 4; © Blend Images/Shutterstock
Images, 6; © aleks.k/Shutterstock Images, 8; © r.martens/Shutterstock
Images, 10; © Artush/Shutterstock Images, 12; © Sergey Uryadnikov/
Shutterstock Images, 14; © seb2583/Shutterstock Images, 16; © Aleksey
Stemmer/Shutterstock Images, 18; © Joost van Uffelen/Shutterstock
Images, 20; © gnomeandi/Shutterstock Images, 20; © Amee Cross/
Shutterstock Images, 20

Library of Congress Cataloging-in-Publication Data
Minden, Cecilia, author.
  Big and small / by Cecilia Minden.
    pages cm.—(Animal opposites)
  Audience: K to grade 3.
  ISBN 978-1-63470-471-7 (hardcover)—ISBN 978-1-63470-591-2 (pbk.)—
ISBN 978-1-63470-531-8 (pdf)—ISBN 978-1-63470-651-3 (ebook)
  1. Animals—Juvenile literature. 2. Body size—Juvenile literature.
3. Concepts—Juvenile literature. 4. Vocabulary. I. Title.
  QL799.3.M56 2016
  590—dc23
                                              2015025720

Cherry Lake Publishing would like to acknowledge
the work of the Partnership for 21st Century Skills.
Please visit www.p21.org for more information.

Printed in the United States of America
Corporate Graphics

TABLE OF CONTENTS

Pets

A dog is big. It likes to go for walks.

What Do You See?

How many goldfish are in the bowl?

A small goldfish likes to swim in a fishbowl.

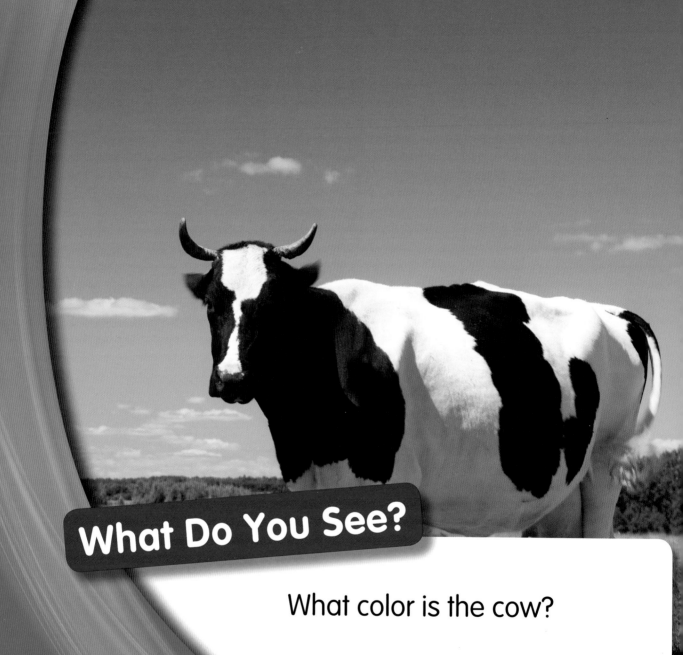

What Do You See?

What color is the cow?

Farm Animals

A big cow needs room to walk and run.

A small **calf** stays next to its mother.

Zoo Animals

An adult **elephant** is big. It has big ears and big feet.

A baby elephant is small. One day, it will be as big as its parents.

Water Animals

A **whale** is very big. It swims in the ocean.

What Do You See?

What is the clown fish doing?

A **clown fish** is small. It likes to swim in the ocean, too.

Which animals are big?

Which animals are small?

Find Out More

BOOK

Horáček, Petr. *Animal Opposites*. Somerville, MA: Candlewick
  Press, 2013.

WEB SITE

The Activity Idea Place—Opposites
www.123child.com/lessonplans/other/opposites.php
Play some games to learn even more opposites.

Glossary

calf (CAF) a baby cow

clown fish (KLOUN fish) a small orange and white fish that lives
in shallow ocean areas

elephant (EL-uh-fuhnt) a large, gray animal with a long trunk
and ivory tusks (long, pointed teeth)

whale (WALE) a large sea animal that looks like a fish but is
actually a mammal that breathes air

Home and School Connection

Use this list of words from the book to help your child become a better reader. Word games and writing activities can help beginning readers reinforce literacy skills.

adult	elephant	parents
an	farm	pets
and	feet	room
are	fish	run
baby	fishbowl	small
big	goldfish	stays
bowl	how	swim
calf	it	the
clown	likes	very
color	many	walk
cow	mother	water
day	needs	whale
dog	next	which
doing	ocean	will
ears	one	zoo

Index

About the Author

Cecilia Minden, PhD, is a former classroom teacher and university professor. She now enjoys working as an educational consultant and writer for school and library publications. She has written more than 150 books for children. Cecilia lives in and out, up and down, and fast and slow in McKinney, Texas.